Twenty L[ove Poems]

and

A Song of Hope in Despair

Mohit Khanduri

Inkfeathers Publishing
www.inkfeathers.com

Twenty Love Poems And A Song of Hope in Despair
Written by Mohit Khanduri
Paperback Edition

First Published in India in 2022
by Inkfeathers Publishing, New Delhi 110095

Copyright © Mohit Khanduri 2022

All rights reserved.
ISBN 9789390882137

Without limiting the rights under copyright reserved above, no part of this publication may be reproduced, lent, resold, or transmitted by any means, electronic, mechanical, photocopying or otherwise, without the prior permission of both the copyright owner and the publisher of this book.

www.inkfeathers.com

Dedicated to

Kaddu

and

My babies (cats) Suppu, Bhuri, Jugnu, Kaalu,
late Laalu-Kaalu and Changu-Mangu

Acknowledgements

I would have never thought to make such a collection had I not read the works of the Chilean poet Pablo Neruda during my undergraduate years. His magnum opus 'Twenty Love Poems and a Song of Despair' gave me the idea for this book. It was love at first sight with the poetry of the Nobel Laureate. Since then, it has been my open-eyed dream to write something like him, and after eight years, one of my dreams has come true.

"I love you as certain dark things are to be loved,
in secret, between the shadow and the soul."

— **Pablo Neruda**

Contents

I	Body of My Woman	1
II	I Love You for Who You Are	3
III	Amy Effect	10
IV	My Polar Star Bright	12
V	I Remember You as You Were	14
VI	Moment by Moment	16
VII	Before Going to Artistic Graves	19
VIII	If I Could Write	21
IX	Full Moon Surrendered	23
X	To My Valentine	26
XI	Under the Shade of a Yellow Flowering Tree	28

XII	The Indian Summer	30
XIII	The Half Sunken Morning	32
XIV	I Have Lost You	35
XV	The Unheard Agony of Heart in a Pitch-Dark Room	39
XVI	Her Last Debt	41
XVII	I Bury My Love	44
XVIII	You Are Far Away	46
XIX	Tonight, I Can Write	49
XX	A Song of Despair	53
	A Song of Hope in Despair	57
	About the Poet	59

Body of My Woman

Body of my woman, glittering amber wrapped in a dusky sheet,
your ethereal beauty hides behind a luxurious facade.
My Amazon! Undiscovered gems, evergreen woods reside in you.
In you flow densest streams as old as mythological isles.

The strength of loins gives rhythm to your amble,
I hold and rub, and bassoon I play on brawny those thighs.
Your mound of Venus, dormant and unruffled,
red-wine lips, amorous but ironical.

The resonance of your mellow voice ripples blood in me,

under that sheeny skin, in liberty, I crawl.

On fast-moving nights, stars count my pulses

and burn to ashes when temptation overrides.

Body of my woman, I will drown in your enticing eyes.

My stimulus, my alpine meadow, my moonlit landscape!

A lush green field where once I grazed,

distance now follows, and darkness prevails.

I Love You for Who You Are

(First love poem composed in the year 2013)

Here I sit with you, my beloved.
As the evening transforms into the night,
at your feet, she awakens.
The usual business of the bazaar, hooting shopkeepers,
and this hustle surrounds us.

In between our conversations, people often intervene,
teenagers are passing by,
seclusion looks grim.
Not many intruders stare at us,
envious some hearts do scorn.

O maid, I am looking at your various shades.

You are the sole observer, the witness of my writing.

Today, see the evolution of your lover,

the formulation of his lines.

Being a downright man, he writes for his joy.

My muse, you are an invisible ink.

Your charisma finds me even in the void,

kajal-filled eyes lit up with delight

on gazing rusty fingers writing a confession swiftly.

With you, I am a whimsical boy.
In your presence, there is a respite from death.
Everything else disappears, oddities expelled,
and I travel in your eyes, seeking no identity or fame.

I was a precious metal buried before you met.
You were an alchemist undertaking a bronze,
showing a defiant will, hands of a wizard,
manifesting wits and satires.

Now I am a malleable mineral, unevenly chastised.
Your squawking refines,
disapproving look illuminates my core
and converts me into pure gold.

A celestial cloth decorates your trunk,
foreseer mouth sings love songs.
Locks you possess, staircases I climb
to reach an immaculately silken face, my paradise.

Truth is beauty, the truth my only God.
Your staunch devotee recites you, my prayer.
My ancestors are a disgrace. I reject their dogmas,
    low-scum thoughts I shed.

O daughter of Lord Brahma, the successor of the multiverse!
    In you, unknown dimensions originate.
With you, I have to go whenever you command.

Bulbs are glowing now. You sparkle like a diamond,

make me kneel and read my intentions.

Is it your disposition which enters me?

With you, clocks run faster; time becomes relative.

Sun abdicates his throne to crown your head,

and the Moon goes down in your nape.

Do not watch me with that alluring face,

the words inside me start to overflow.

O power of Neptune, say something, sweep me off my feet.

When conformists equate love to sin, dictators
> preach democracy.
> I am a shepherd carrying a cat or a lamb,
> > declaring you my only religion.

> > > I love you for who you are
> > > I love you for your craft, Athena.
> > > My salvation resides in you.

Amy Effect

(Composed for a princess on 21 September 2020)

The princess of the city of temples!

Your ruling deity tied the holiest river in his hair coiled.

Sinners fear his eye of destruction,

ignorant of your wrath that scares me the most.

A peacock's tears flow like a river

to fertilise the ancestors' land.

My oppressed heart takes refuge in you,

shackles of submission break into pieces.

Your voluptuous voice stirs artistry,

the magic of aura invades my nights.

Fog accumulates around your slender waist
as clouds of twilight,
mist drips slowly from that waistline.
Saffron sunbeams falling upon your face
heal my soul's wounds opened in solitude.

Let me drink from your immortal mouth filled with
drunken bees.
You are the intellect of the century
surpassing our contemporaries.
My nemesis! Had our soliloquies ever come out,
what would have happened to the intelligentsia?

My Polar Star Bright

You are an ideal of solemn beauty
tempting me through your intense affection.
Dangling earrings crown your patient ears,
eyes shimmer like crystal clear lakes,
flushed cheeks shake as Canterbury bells.

Sun had left the horizon,
and the moon was yet to come.
You became my navigator, my polar star bright.
Falling in love is subtle.
It began to quiver us.

How was it my lady
to be kissed on a bewitching neck?
Delicate earlobes pulled warm lips,
you got titillated.
Imprints now they bear.

Hands explored, a nymph laid bare,
musk from her glands left no choice,
speechless senses embarked on an ecstatic state.
High hills stood against my chest, ready to go.
My raw vegetable, I devoured you slow.

A breeze blew so strong
that your eyes gliding in the seventh sky opened.
Enclosing the boy, you whispered with a bite, "Be
my cover."
Like a sculptor, I carved my clay.

I Remember You As You Were

I remember you as you were:

a glaring sunray vanishing in the winter of the year we parted.

The colossal youth collapsed.

I shared my childhood with the psyche of your girlhood,

and wandered in the universe, the mass of your eyes.

Crystallization of love exists in me.

Like a grapevine, I clung to your soul.

Fire your essence colonised my heart

to rule over still water, my quintessence.

We discovered each other, rosy dawn arose,
infinite colours came from a dazzling explosion,
your godly body shone luminously.
Oh, the garden of pubis! The fragrance of your tulips!

From the wilderness of your naturism,
unfulfilled yearnings came upon the surface.
Ageing neither to rue nor to wait,
your tenacity and ardour kept the spark.

Moist eyes pleaded every day to hear from you
what I wanted to say.
Naivety met an invincible force,
stellar this union resolved anguished complaints.

Moment by Moment

(Inspired by the poem *I carry your heart with me* by E. E. Cummings)

Moment by moment, I love you
and carry you within my heart.
As the moments grow into years,
sufferings in love inflicted upon me
nourish the seed of art.

Wounds of love carelessly rupture;
passions turn this hopelessness into a golden notebook.
In the twilight red sky, queerish manoeuvrings,
our camaraderie is persistent.

They see you as my guide, the torchbearer,
unaware of the stabbing. I was not Caesar, my love.
What countless things can a female loath?
In your heart, berries of love will sprout.

In my eyes, the flickering constellation Orion you see.
In your eyes, Sirius the brightest shines.
My bright star!
From the prominent constellations
descend meteors and comets to grace our bond.

Wherever you are, remember the lines:
As the summers pass, glaciers become snow-laden,
my body metamorphoses into a resolute statue.

Send radio signals from your eyes,
cold as space, hot as the sun.
You are the Goddess of Astronomy,
you are Aries born on Mars.

The last present that I owe to you is my heart.
When I leave the nation of migrants,
cut out my chest and take out the heart
that releases your energy.
It culminates in you.

Moment by moment, I love you
and carry you within my heart.

Before Going to Artistic Graves

Cold winds win my body,
I go quiet under a quilt.
Take me over and give me the warmth of love,
Let me wear your wild aroma.

The last snowfall of the season has thrown down
an avalanche on me.
Protect me from this nippy weather,
take me inside my temple.
Let your body sweat for some time.

Sensations run through your spine,
the body shivers, and kisses arouse it.
Turn around, turn around, angel.
I will sow some seeds.

The vast plain from north to south,
whatever is hidden, unveil!
Before going to artistic graves,
let us burn ourselves.

If I Could Write

(Inspired from the poem *If I Could Tell You*
by W.H. Auden)

You will say nothing, but I told you so,
No generation knows what I reminisce between us.
If I could write, I would let you know.

If we should brood when lovers are in spirits low,
If we should stop when cupids do not play,
You will say nothing, but I told you so.

Past is the glory when our bodies moved to and fro,
You dote upon cloudy days; I cherish the sunny ones.
If I could write, I would let you know.

The days of betrayal were long, nights never so slow,

I am a corpse now for whom cuckoos do not sing.

You will say nothing, but I told you so.

I stayed and loved less, never enough to show,

There were umpteen things I wanted to do,

If I could write, I would let you know.

I live now somewhere where plants never grow.

Your slavery was freedom, freedom now slavery of life.

Will you say nothing, even if I told you to?

If I could write, I would let you know.

Full Moon Surrendered

Twinkling stars were alone on a New Moon night,
    My full moon was surrendering in lap mine.
    Crickets were chirping for the longest night,
        merry must be they and wooing their wise.

        Your neck took a long back flight,
      marks on the neck dug deep by dive.
    Flawless callous bosoms, swollen and ripe,
        luring abdomen felt cold lips mine.

My love, time flies on a chariot faster than light.
          Beauty is not to turn to ashes;
        your virgin vault is not to pry.
      Kisses drizzled; coyness left aside.

From the supple midriff, I leaned narrow.
Plumpy sandalwood legs had spread out,
I saw a carpel and a pink stigma.
Nothing was left to think or hide.

Bodies constrained by low minds got free,
and pristine your caves called me in.
Synchronised hearts learned to fly
like a roller coaster adventure-seekers ride.

You muttered some words. I read that mumbling.
The clock struck midnight,
intoxicated minds obeyed caged instincts
to soak the rarest joy.

When your moaning hands pushed me in,
loosened wet walls liberated our spirits.
Was it a divine blessing or sensual bliss?
No one could ever know.

Blazing organs absorbed this fervour,
weary bodies suddenly groaned.
Stagnated a pond gave away a rill.
Could you not hold the fluids, my love?

The night was delighted,
and the morning came to knock on the door.
You said, "Go now. Later, I will call."
She walked away quietly.

Earthlings are waking. Let us sleep,
gently will pass frolicsome next night.
Let come the eve, my love!
We will go for a walk by the Ganga's side.

To My Valentine

(Composed on 14 February 2019)

The first drizzle of the spring bathes frozen lands,

shredding leaves wither to become a compost pile.

Bumblebees venture out for nectar and pollen,

to build a new home, mate, and hatch eggs.

Here, my soaring heartache urges for some zing.

Pansies and peonies welcome you, night-blooming Jasmine!

Hyacinth and lilies bloom, and cherries turn red.

Your florid face, couplets of epics in rhymes,

and infinite times I want to kiss your placid eyes.

Those snoozing eyes are most pleasing to my lonely heart.

A bough of blue roses adorns your swan neck,
and the necklace of pearls falls upon the breast.
My coward fingers caress those cheeks, petals of Camellia,
tickle you everywhere by moving like a snake.
Alas! I cannot lie beside you, Valentine.

In the rain falling outside, I longed to be with her,
to get drenched together.
I must quench my thirst:
One is calling out, and the other calls from inside.
Does she fancy any luck?

My sunshine, my sleeping bride! Remain under that blanket,
or rise from your sleep to enfold me in your arms.
Celebrate your life, be joyful as I am.
I have sent cuddles and the toing-toing thing we do,
and all the love I could have sent.

Under the Shade of a Yellow Flowering Tree

Under the shade of a yellow flowering tree
the enigmatic smile of a girl enslaves men,
lessens magnificence of stoic flowers
wanting animosity.

The enchantress harvests richness, her suitor, a destitute.
O ageless face bearer, the colour of daffodils!
You stand there, holding a flower like a dragon-warrior
in a black cloak coat and knee-high boots.

A Baudelaire bag hangs from your shoulder,
keeping feminine treasures.

You are a countryside view.

Let me lose my fanatic heart, possessions that I have,

let me paint you through the eyes of a doll.

What do I see in her:

Starry eyes or pragmatic thoughts?

The yellow background is happy escapism, a fleeting impression,

an illusion relived.

My Cleopatra reigns in a brave new world with poisonous eyes,

astute her will moves Jupiter's storms.

Ignominious dreams of a shattered soul

wait for her benevolence.

The Indian Summer

(Love could not resist Chaucer and T S Eliot)

The Indian summer begins in April.
On the first of April, once nineteen pilgrims took off,
nine praised seven sins, repentance ignored,
four gave up their souls to worship Satan.

Tests of devotion passed, three got martyrdom.
November came, the pilgrimage became harsh,
two women vanished with no clue,
and one pilgrim reached, at last.

On English land, it may be the cruellest month,
reproducing hollow men in the wasteland,
April regenerates everything on Indian land.

Life is born out of chaos,
showers abundance on lands infertile
and herbs unheard burgeon everywhere.

Aye, she accompanied sixteen seasons,
four breezing summers' pleasures relished,
before disappearing into a green valley.

Indian summer breaks blockades for all.
Cumulus clouds hide April's mountains,
Himalayan blue poppies cover her foothills.

Years have gone by, an ache prolonged.
Like a wood plank, I drift into you, my sea.
In your eyes, I will live my saviour.
In your blood, I get dissolved.

The Half Sunken Morning

The cure for pain is in pain.
—Rumi

I am the loneliest station somewhere on the South Pole.

Languorous mornings seize me throughout the day

Dejected evenings throw me into the pit of self-hatred.

You are my polar ice comforting in polar summer.

Sometimes, your love was a tropical region.

Sometimes, exotic places filled with prospered nature.

In the quietness of the closed bazaar,

dew on our lips wished their greetings.

The chills of 8 AM made us sit on dirty floors.

I listened, gazed at a face not embellished with creams.

You made a reticent pair to read *Rumi*.

I kissed your forehead, held a kind hand,

and in those dreamlike moments, your monologues poured *Amrit* on me.

My verses' language stemmed from *tasawwuf*.

O, *Sufi* mystic! Receive offerings, the hymns that I sing.

Leaving behind worldly pleasures and traditions extreme,

this *fakir* submits his repressed soul.

Annotations:

Rumi: A thirteenth century Persian poet and Sufi mystic originally from Greater Iran. His poems have been widely translated into many of the world's languages

Amrit: A Sanskrit word that means "immortality". In Hinduism, it is often referred to in ancient Indian texts as an elixir

Tasawwuff : Tasawwuf is an Arabic term for the process of realizing ethical and spiritual ideals, meaning literally "becoming a Sufi," *tasawwuf* is generally translated as Sufism

Sufi: A person who is adherent to mystic orders or teachings, and emphasise the direct experience of God

Faqir: A religious ascetic who lives solely on alms

I Have Lost You

I have lost you, my woman.
You are the new monarch
whom the commoners do not know.

I liked you as you were:
a fluttering bee sprinkling the pollens of
imagination
onto white sheets.
The sketches you reap
come out of the land of your labour.
Intricate drawings with microscopic details,
the identity of a prodigy beneath her disguise.

Your body is the tree of revolutions,
unripe fruits you bear.
Sweet and sour juices leak from that sturdy flesh,
and a luscious throat craves mad kisses.
How could I have not loved pitiless spongy domes,
beguiling windows to my heartstrings?

Your vivacity flings unmeasurable aeons,
lord of the creation is submissive to your whims.
Her fuming face invites annihilation,
sends storms in the West,
earthquakes in the East.

Never was I barred from going into my dormitory.
How I would keep my head,
where pillows of your breast I got to sleep.
You threw yourself surreptitiously in my arms,
felt my naked body, naked soul.

The exploiters of pleasures don't see
the wailings of the hearts
carrying the enlightenment for the human race.
In you, everything disintegrates
to reunite with the creator.

An odyssey of emotions I undertook
in that macrocosm
and plunged in to feel every relief.
Thousands of identities flourish within her.

She is an infallible human,
the descendant of goddess Kali.
Her pellucid eyes reflect the kingdom of Shambhala,
absolute a place
where I met Kalki avatar.

Propitious her expressions are Utopia's visions
expressing her life, vibrating persona.
How can one measure a woman's heart?
The oldest secrets dwell there.

Her dilated pupils comprehend an imminent act
and compel me to renounce other desires, the
cause of my ordeals.
Soaking her energy makes me non-human.
Did I attain Nirvana?

The Unheard Agony of Heart in a Pitch-Dark Room

Until the last drop of my tear does not leave my face
numb with the wetness of tears,
until the water inside my body does not evaporate
to make the body a desert-like Sahara,
sandy winds will howl in pain,
I will weep, and I will cry.

Until your remembrance does not reduce itself
to an involuntary process,
no further in my control,
I will weep, and I will cry.

Until the last star, the last atom of hydrogen
and the solar systems do not deplete,
until the existence of nebulas or a black hole,
I will weep, and I will cry.

Maybe a gigantic explosion made the cosmos,
and left it as such,
my love for you was material-less,
never created or destroyed.

Her Last Debt

Since she, whom I love,
had paid her last debt by leaving me,
I cannot breathe again as free as a bird,
endless as the sky.
In lonely summer nights
owls come to chatter
and whine gusty winds.

Neither one step moved ahead nor behind.
I stand at the crossroad from where you disappeared.
Humans are not born to accumulate everything,
earn and spend to express their lives.

Man is hungry for man's blood,
I confront fear, the master from whom you run
will tell my master to give me freedom
or dictate this miserable life until I die.

What makes you think I don't care?
Neither you pardon nor is it fair.
Last we stopped at a hostel
where you said, "I never care."

I drove six miles to reach my end
without getting mowed.
That murderous night of mid-December
recurs every day.
Our time is gone, history forgotten,
and sea waves crashing on my rock-like heart
become a painful sight.

You compete. I walk on the path I chose.
One cannot take both roads,
lies a saga in between those roads
that silently speaks.
Let them hear.

I Bury My Love

It may be the last verse I write for you,
or the final verse for our knot
as burying my love is easy now.

The heads in the graveyard sob,
an end that people mourn.
The funeral has begun.
I give sermons, read love letters,
a white shroud I draw and perform last rites.
Without chanting *shlokas*, I complete every ritual.

My pain comes out of my eyes to meet the soil
full of your footprints which cleansed the earth.
The strangers leave one by one.

In my solitary part now, flowers purple I throw
and throw loam on this tomb
as burying my love is easy now.

The epitaph reads: Here lies the man who lived in
poetry,
and in whom poetry lived.
I will endure your fury,
the apocalypse in the heaven you brought
somehow.

You Are Far Away

You are far away, farther than everything,

moving faster than the speed of light.

You violate rules of matter and time at will.

There is no way to sense your presence, enter into your realm,

I know you as an unseen particle with no permanent stay.

You can be seen and loved only in imagination,

like a revered apostle, a forbidden apple.

My uncanny mind does make you irrespective of what I contemplate:

Modus operandi of tying hair, clothes you could wear,

and rapturous eyes that teach hard lessons.

You, the epitome of discernment, restrict
everything against immortality,

in the journey of inferno, loving you was my only
crime.

With ageing, poets become sad as adversities give
them bitter wisdom,

they cannot see their species tearing itself apart,

chasing illusions of truth as opposed to the
polemics of agnostic philosophers.

My youthful days lie behind,

I do not have anything to rejoice, anything that can
excite me.

Soon, like an extinct river, I will recede,

unlike you, my game, my pain, my paramour.

Give me a chance to say the ramblings of my mind;

years have gone by while living in the sea of your fear.

Cosmic messages float in the air of your demeanour,

beneath my unsaid words, I prefer a sudden demise.

Objects around me will remember you

for doing most of the things with me on the earth,

consuming me in your thoughts, loving me surreal,

and being loved much the same by me.

Tonight, I Can Write

(Composed on 15 August 2018)

Neruda! *What you wrote, I cannot*
Give my pen the strength to cease not.

Tonight, I can write the saddest lines
when the sky for stars, as for her, my soul pines.
Not only did I love her, but she loved me too.
The love we made toiled on our skin,
scintillating my cells, she gave me a grin.

She liked to play games of tongues,

I used to suck honey dripping from her lips.

Those magnetic eyes I fell for, and silvery her eyelids.

It has been ages since she left.

Still, her odour pervades me but makes summer evenings love bereft.

Once lost in her galactic eyes, I would never come back.

Sweet kisses on her ears; she imparted thousands on my neck.

The grief of separation is less, of everlasting memories more.

How she came into my life, a lucent dress she wore.

She was my Himalayas, my panoramic view.

Whenever I stroked her glossy hairs and navel firm,

the indomitable girl became fluffy as snow,

lilting sounds would come with her flow.

Oh, that blush! Those bubbles of condensed moisture on her nose!

And she would turn into a blossoming rose.

You were searching for the saddest lines,

I wrote you the happiest rhymes.

Find those saddest lines inside a house

where no sunlight dares to visit,

a desolated bleak shed in a barren land.

A dead tree in the middle of the veranda,
no leaves in it.
A house with rooms but no roof,
the hottest spot on the planet
releasing the sun's heat from a burning pyre.

A Song of Despair

Dusk has fallen. Your memory imprisons me like every other day.

In my silhouette, muted is your laugh,

and like every other night, years crumble under their plight.

I have come to a halt to call you in empty fields, plateaus and ghats.

Leaving his testament, a dead lover departs.

Look into my gloomy eyes, a melancholy heart,

every word you spoke, every day we passed, they too depart.

Where are you, my song? Raindrops fall, and there is no sound.

On the last voyage with a broken compass, the ship of my life has left its port.

I don't recall those long evening walks or sitting by your side,

but can Moon be stopped from bringing high tides?

You are the palace stood on a holy Sangam, three rivers you swallow,

saints and monks, priests and preachers are startled.

I made a monument of grief and tormented its cries.

You are its history, the strength of the marble, and I am its shadow.

Night creatures visit me. Like a wolf, they growl and haunt.

My lifeless body chooses you as my soul chooses these pages to stroll.

My peak! My prestige! My Queen undeclared of every empire!

Away from the masquerading of the world, you are my carnival.

Nature keeps me in harmony shaping my character,

you taught me ambitions and first fight against my bondage.

The seven wonders salute you in awe.

You are above them; my poetic diction reduces the grandeur of their past.

O lost medicine woman, the foundation of my works!

Black furs you liked; you are the arguments of law I loved.

Ah! You have gone for too long now.

Unimaginable scenes float, seeing you in someone else's arms.

You will choose another man but during the hour of lament,

thousands of my births, every reincarnation will be massacred.

I have chosen you, the first and the last.

Be my heir. To you, every right of my verse I pass.

Oh, my emerald! My emerald! I have to go now to follow the sinking sun.

My longing to live for you has died.

A Song of Hope in Despair

My wait for you sets every night, then rises again.
                One day, I will cease to exist.
The stiff body will erode in a somber atmosphere,
        the grey dust in the air will smell lavender.

Hope is the flame of patience, the most beautiful
                            thing
in which I get parched between you and my doom
          to watch the green sun rising in my life,
          intuition ignoring skepticism of thoughts.

            Slam the door, and there will be a thud.
            I will behold the keeper of a *Jyotirlinga*.
    Do not let me suppress my tears, run along the
                                  way.
                Your gestures are enough to speak.
                        I will resurrect.

Don't fret, inamorata. There is no turning back,
end this interlude between us.
Its boundless extension has devasted companions
and shaken their faith.
Butterflies have left cities in turmoil.

You are the aesthetic mirror reflecting my image.
People around me in thousands or a few,
two hearts will conjoin,
thousands will melt.
Else in obscurity, I will be at peace.

Annotations:

Jyotirlinga: A Jyotirlinga or Jyotirlingam is a devotional representation of the Hindu god Shiva.

About the Poet

Mohit Khanduri was born and bred in Garhwal for the first five years and did his schooling in Dehradun. Mountains, snowfall, wanderings in dense forests, and brooks and rivers shaped his imagination and creativity. He completed B.A. (Honours) English from the University of Delhi before taking a master's degree from Jamia Millia Islamia, New Delhi. P. B. Shelley, John Keats and Pablo Neruda are his favorite poets. He is a bilingual writer who has also written traditional verses and short stories.

INKFEATHERS PUBLISHING

India's Most Author Friendly Publishing House

Stay updated about the latest books, anthologies, events, exclusive offers, contests, product giveaways and other things that we do to support authors.

 Inkfeathers Publishing

 @InkfeathersPublishing

 @_Inkfeathers

 @Inkfeathers

 Inkfeathers.com

We'd love to connect with you!

Printed in Great Britain
by Amazon